Paul Strathern

WITTGENSTEIN
(1889–1951)
in 90 minutes

Constable · London

First published in Great Britain 1996
by Constable and Company Limited
3 The Lanchesters, 162 Fulham Palace Road
London W6 9ER
Copyright © Paul Strathern 1996
The right of Paul Strathern to be identified as author
of this work has been asserted by him
in accordance with the Copyright,
Designs and Patents Act 1988
ISBN 0 09 475970 7
Set in Linotron Sabon by
Rowland Phototypesetting Ltd,
Bury St Edmunds, Suffolk
Printed in Great Britain by
St Edmundsbury Press Ltd,
Bury St Edmunds, Suffolk

A CIP catalogue record of this book
is available from the British Library

Contents

Contents

Introduction

If we accept Wittgenstein's word for it, he is the last philosopher. In his view, philosophy in the traditional sense – as it had been known in the twenty-five centuries since it was started by the Ancient Greeks – was finished. After what he had done to philosophy, it was no longer possible.

It is fitting that philosophy should end with its most limited practitioner. Ludwig Wittgenstein was a superb logician, and his solution to the problems of philosophy was to reduce them to logic. All else was excluded – metaphysics, aesthetics, ethics, finally even philosophy itself. Wittgenstein sought the 'final solution' for philosophy, with the aim of putting an end to it once and for all. He had one go at this, but it didn't work; so he had a second try, which did.

Life and work

Apart perhaps from Leibnitz, Wittgenstein is the only major philosopher to have produced two distinct philosophies. And when one considers that both of these were dedicated to finishing off philosophy, one begins to get a measure of the man's perverse dedication.

Obviously Father had something to do with this. It is appropriate that Wittgenstein grew up just across town from where Sigmund Freud had recently installed the world's most famous couch. Wittgenstein's father Karl was a tyrant. By the time young Ludwig arrived on the scene his father was one of the uncrowned industrial kings of Europe (more powerful even than Krupp) and a predominating influence on the Viennese cultural scene (Brahms would play at home after dinner, and in the art world Karl Wittgenstein personally founded the Vienna Sezession). Karl

Wittgenstein had a domineering personality, first-class intellect, a deep understanding of culture, was brimming with self-assurance and could charm the birds from the trees (on the days when he didn't feel like blasting them off the branches). The effect on his family was catastrophic. Young Ludwig had four older brothers, the majority of whom appear to have been brilliant, exceptionally highly strung, and homosexual. Three of them were to commit suicide – a possibility which Ludwig clung to like a talisman throughout his life. The other brother who survived became a concert pianist, had his right hand blown off in the First World War, and afterwards continued with his career – commissioning piano concertos for the left hand, including the celebrated one by Ravel. He was not considered to have been so brilliant as his other brothers, or even the best pianist.

Ludwig Wittgenstein was born in Vienna on 26 April 1889 and brought up in a palace on the exclusive Alleegasse (now Argentinier-strasse), which runs between the Ringstrasse and the Südbahnhof. Here Wittgenstein was educated by private tutors amidst an atmosphere of extreme cultural intensity (suicidal genius brothers practised at the grand piano long into the early hours, a sister commissioned her portrait by Klimt and rejected the Goyas from the family collection because 'their tone was out of place'). At the age of ten young Ludwig singlehandedly designed and constructed out of pieces of wood and wire a working model sewing-machine. By the time he was fourteen he could whistle entire movements from a number of well-known symphonies. These activities would seem to be the nearest he came to playing in the manner of an ordinary child.

In 1903 Wittgenstein left home for the first time to attend the Realschule in Linz, where he studied mathematics and science. Curiously, Hitler was at this school at the same time.

They were both the same age, and should have studied in the same class. Wittgenstein considered that he was a mediocre student, but was nonetheless promoted to the year above his age group; Hitler records how he shone amongst his doltish classmates, but according to the records was kept back in the year lower than his age group – so the mediocrity and the supreme genius never met.

After this Wittgenstein studied mechanical engineering for two years at the Technische Hochschule at Charlottenburg in Berlin; and in 1908 he left to continue his studies in England. For the next three years he did research in aeronautics at Manchester University, and conducted experiments with kites at the Upper Atmosphere Station near Glossop in Derbyshire. At this stage Wittgenstein still showed no sign of what was to come. He knew nothing about philosophy, and was considered *quite* bright (certainly not brilliant) by his colleagues. In the typical English manner of the period Wittgenstein's colleagues tended to regard him merely as an eccentric German. They were wrong: he was an eccentric Austrian – a rare, but altogether more idiosyncratic breed. Wittgenstein was punctiliously well-mannered, yet capable of flying into a storming rage when anything went wrong with his experiments. In his relations with others he conveyed a cosmopolitan Viennese polish, but it soon became apparent to his colleagues that he hadn't the first idea of how to get along socially with ordinary people (i.e. anyone other than the geniuses, magnates and statesmen who frequented the Palais Wittgenstein). He would work fanatically all day without a single break, and then lie in a scalding bath all evening contemplating suicide. One Sunday when he wanted to go to Blackpool with a colleague and they missed the train, Wittgenstein suggested that they should hire one for the two of them.

As part of his research, Wittgenstein set

about designing a propeller. The problems posed by this led him into mathematical theory. This appears to have triggered some unconscious impulse in Wittgenstein. Within a remarkably short time his intellect focused, assuming all the power of his intense personality. The propeller and its attendant mathematics were soon forgotten as he continued questioning ever more deeply, until eventually he was probing the very foundations of mathematics. It was as if his mind had locked onto the need to discover some utter bedrock of certainty in the world. It is perhaps no accident that around this time his brothers started comitting suicide and his father became terminally ill with cancer.

Who knew about the foundations of mathematics? Wittgenstein was told of the recent pioneering work done by Bertrand Russell, and immediately began reading his *Principles of Mathematics*, the very latest work on the subject. In this, Russell set out to prove that the fundamentals of mathematics were in fact logical, and that all pure mathematics could be derived from a few basic logical principles. However, Russell's attempt foundered on a paradox. Russell tried to define number by using classes. Some classes are members of themselves, and some are not. For example, the class of human beings is not a member of itself because it is not a human being. However, the class of non-human beings is a member of itself. But is the class of all classes which are not members of themselves, a member of itself? If it is, it is not. Yet if it is not, it is. The entire status of mathematics hung on this Christmas cracker paradox, which according to Russell affected 'the very foundations of reasoning'. He ended his book by issuing a challenge to 'all students of logic' to solve it. Wittgenstein immediately decided that he was a member of this class which was not a member of itself, and launched into the fray. He came up with a radical solution, dismissing the entire concept of classes as an unwarranted assumption.

Russell in his turn dismissed Wittgenstein's solution, while at the same time admiring its ingenuity. But Wittgenstein was not so easily put off. In 1911 he travelled to Cambridge to see Russell. He immediately decided to study philosophy with Russell and abandon engineering (the profession which his father had chosen for him: young Ludwig was to be the *useful* member of the family).

Russell had taken on a lot more than he'd bargained for. At the time Russell was arguably the leading philosopher in Europe; Wittgenstein had only read one book on the subject (and that was more mathematics than it was philosophy). Yet Wittgenstein took to arriving in Russell's rooms at all times of day and night, and insisted upon engaging him for hours on end in the most intense 'philosophical' speculations – sometimes to do with logic, sometimes to do with suicide. According to Russell,

Wittgenstein had 'passion and vehemence' and a feeling that 'one must understand or die'. Yet when he was convinced that he did understand, nothing would convince him to the contrary. He refused to accept Russell's belief in empiricism: that we can learn knowledge from our experience. In Wittgenstein's view knowledge was limited to logic. When Russell claimed that he knew there was no rhinoceros in the room, Wittgenstein refused to accept this. It was logically possible that there *was* a rhinoceros in the room. Russell then asked him where this rhinoceros could possibly be, and began looking behind the chairs and under the table. But still Wittgenstein adamantly refused to accept that Russell knew for certain that there was no rhinoceros in the room.

Fortunately (or perhaps unfortunately for philosophy) Russell quickly realized that his impossibly intense and egotistical new student was more than just an obstinate pestering bore. But he also realized that his new student needed to learn some basic logic. At some inconvenience, Russell used his influence and arranged for Wittgenstein to be tutored by a leading Cambridge logician, W. E. Johnson, a fellow of Kings College. The result was a fiasco. 'I found in the first hour that he had nothing to teach me,' declared Wittgenstein. Johnson ironically observed: 'At our first meeting he was teaching me.' This arrogant rudeness and inability to listen were to become an increasingly dominant trait in Wittgenstein's character.

Russell generously characterized this period of getting to know Wittgenstein as 'one of the most exciting intellectual adventures of my life'. He and Wittgenstein began discussing mathematical logic, which at the time was so complex that only half a dozen people in the world could understand it. Yet according to Russell, within two years Wittgenstein 'knew all I had to teach'. More than this, Wittgenstein had managed to convince Russell that he would never do any creative philosophy again. It was too difficult for him. Only he, Wittgenstein, could possibly discover the way forward.

Wittgenstein had found a substitute father – and destroyed him. Fortunately Wittgenstein's intellect was just as powerful as his personality. Indeed it's almost impossible to separate the two, and both had now found their purpose in life. This was more than just a psychological hatchet job by Wittgenstein. The only thing that could stop him from destroying everything, including himself, was the 'truth'.

It is no exaggeration to compare Wittgenstein wrestling with the problems of logic to Jacob wrestling with his angel. As soon as Wittgenstein discovered philosophy, it became a matter of life and death for him, and anyone who felt it as less than this was viewed with contempt. But this period of self-realization also led to some rather less exalted discoveries. Wittgenstein realized that he was homosexual. He enjoyed spending his time in intense conversation with lonely intellectual young men, but couldn't bring himself to sully these relationships with any sensuality. This element in his nature was almost certainly relieved by rare visits to London, or occasional night pick-ups in the Prater, the main park in Vienna, when he went home. All this only contributed to his psychological turmoil. Here was daemonic genius at its purest – aspiring to the heights, yet living in shadow, driven to the point where it was all but out of control. After Wittgenstein's father finally died ('the most beautiful death that I can imagine, falling asleep like a child'), he headed back to Cambridge to do battle against the problem of logic with renewed vigour.

Yet there were moments of comparative bliss. In 1913 Wittgenstein went with his friend, the gifted young mathematician David

Pinsent, on a summer holiday to Norway. Here the two of them often enjoyed themselves like thirteen-year-old schoolboys. But Wittgenstein could be an exacting travelling companion, even for an easy-going self-effacing character like Pinsent. Each morning Wittgenstein insisted on doing logic for several hours. In Pinsent's words: 'When he is working he mutters to himself (in a mixture of German and English) and strides up and down all the while.' At other times he was liable to take extreme offence over trifles. When Pinsent stopped to take a photograph of the scenery, or even spoke to someone else on a train, this would provoke an emotional outburst, followed by a long fit of the sulks. It is difficult to gauge how much this stemmed from Wittgenstein's overriding need to dominate, and how much was due to lover's jealousy (or other unspoken conflicts arising from his unspoken love).

Wittgenstein grew increasingly eccentric

and neurotic. As the holiday progressed he became convinced that he was going to die, and kept harping on this to Pinsent, who concluded 'he was mad'. By now Wittgenstein was breaking new ground in logic, and felt he was close to solving the problems which had prevented Russell from discovering the logical foundation for mathematics. The only trouble was that he now felt sure he would die before he could publish the truth. Wittgenstein wrote to Russell, demanding that they meet 'as soon as possible', so that Wittgenstein could tell him where he had gone wrong.

Despite all this, when they returned to England Wittgenstein informed Pinsent that this was the best holiday he had ever had. In the understatement of a true Englishman, Pinsent confided to his diary that Wittgenstein had been 'trying at times', but had enough sense to promise himself that he would never go on holiday with him again.

Meanwhile Wittgenstein was having a

series of urgent meetings with Russell. Wittgenstein was in an excited state, and Russell found it impossible to follow his complex logical arguments. But Russell became even more exasperated when Wittgenstein refused to commit himself to paper until he had brought his ideas to perfection. In the end Russell managed to persuade Wittgenstein to let a stenographer be present at their meetings, so that Wittgenstein's answers to Russell's probing questions could be taken down in shorthand.

These notes form the basis of Wittgenstein's first work: *Notes on Logic*. In this Wittgenstein makes numerous insightful remarks, some of breathtaking simplicity (such as: '"A" is the same as the letter "A".') Russell understood at once what Wittgenstein was trying to establish: in order to overcome the paradoxical difficulties, things needed to be *shown* in symbolic form, rather than *said* (because they simply could not be said, and were in fact unsayable). This was difficult to grasp at the best of times. Indeed, it is probable that only Russell really understood what Wittgenstein was getting at. And it looked like remaining that way, for as Russell said: 'I told him he ought not simply to *state* what he thinks true, but to give arguments for it, but he said arguments spoil its beauty, and that he would feel as if he was dirtying a flower with muddy hands.' Wittgenstein was a perfectionist: either you understood perfectly, completely and at once what he said, or there was no point in listening to what he said at all.

However, in this unpublished work Wittgenstein did also include certain ideas he had about philosophy. These are remarkable for their originality: no one was thinking like this in 1912. And they also contain the conception of philosophy which he was to retain throughout his life: 'In philosophy there are no deductions: *it* is purely descriptive.' According to Wittgenstein philosophy gave no picture of reality, and it neither confirmed nor confuted scientific investigation. 'Philosophy consists of logic and metaphysics: logic is its basis.' It appeared to have little connection with reality, and was more concerned with the study of language. 'Distrust of grammar is the first requisite for philosophizing.'

Wittgenstein had identified philosophy with logic. Here, in embryo, was much of his later philosophy. It could be said that from now on he devoted his life to elaborating these remarks and their implications. But before embarking upon his new philosophy, Wittgenstein decided that perhaps it was time he began studying some philosophy. There was no harm in finding out what others had been up to. According to Pinsent: 'Wittgenstein has only just started systematic reading "in philosophy" and he expresses the most naïve surprise that all the philosophers he once worshipped in ignorance are after all stupid and dishonest and make disgusting mistakes.' So much for the opposition.

Wittgenstein now decided that the only thing for him to do was return to Norway, and live in isolation for the next two years 'doing logic'. Even by Wittgenstein's standards, this was somewhat drastic. According to the superb biography of Wittgenstein by Ray Monk, Russell thought this idea 'wild and lunatic'. He tried his best to dissuade Wittgenstein: 'I said it would be dark, & he said he hated daylight. I said it would be lonely, & he said he prostituted his mind talking to intelligent people. I said he was mad & he said God preserve him from sanity. (God certainly will.)'

Pinsent was deeply saddened at their farewell. (Though neither of them had the slightest inkling, this was to be their final parting.) Even Wittgenstein seems to have been peripherally perplexed at his decision, but was nonetheless absolutely determined to go through with it.

Wittgenstein duly sailed to Norway, and soon found just the place he was looking for.

This was a hut ninety miles up the Hardanger fjord, which could only be reached by rowing boat from the remote village of Skjolden. It is difficult to conceive of anywhere in Europe further removed from the sophisticated splendours in which he had been brought up – and this was probably the point.

Wittgenstein now embarked upon a long, cold, dark winter of utter solitude 'doing logic'. Not surprisingly, he was soon writing to Russell: 'I often think I am going mad.' But his letters to Russell also contained evidence of the startling advances he was making in logic. These follow directly from Russell's attempt to discover a logical foundation for mathematics, but go even further – attempting to discover a foundation for logic itself.

Wittgenstein asserted that a logical proposition could be shown to be true or false regardless of its constituent parts. For instance, if we say: 'This apple is red or not red' this is a tautology (i.e. it is always true). And it will always be true regardless of whether the apple is red or not. Likewise, if we say: 'This apple is neither red nor not red' this is a contradiction (i.e. it will always be false). If we had a method for finding out whether a logical proposition is a tautology, or a contradiction, or neither, then we would have a rule for determining the truth of all propositions. This rule, stated as a proposition, would be the basis of all logic.

Wittgenstein would never have returned to civilization for anything so trivial as to protect his sanity. However, when he heard that his mother was ailing he felt obliged to travel to Vienna. On his arrival he found that he had inherited a fortune. But he didn't want his life to be encumbered with Wittgenstein money, and decided to give it away. He started by making donations, anonymously, to a number of Austrian poets. His choice of recipients was revealing: one was Rilke, whose cultivated lyrics expressed an intense spirituality, and another was Trakl, who hymned his obsession with guilt and decline in a series of dark enigmatic images.

At the outbreak of the First World War Wittgenstein joined up in the Austro-Hungarian army. He learned that his beloved Pinsent had joined up on the opposing side. Wittgenstein didn't enlist because he particularly believed in the cause of the German powers, but because he felt it was his duty. As a Wittgenstein he could easily have become an officer, but he chose to remain in the ranks – an extremely dangerous decision. This was the farcically inefficient army of Hasek's *The Good Soldier Svejk* – the army whose eastern commander was to despatch the immortal telegram: 'The situation is hopeless but not desperate.' Wittgenstein was sent to fight against the Russians on the Eastern Front, where the carnage matched that of the trenches on the Western Front in France. To begin with he served on a river gunboat in Galicia, then with an artillery battery. Throughout this period Wittgenstein continued to write down his philosophical ideas in notebooks. He was doing original philosophy, but he also remained constantly on the brink of suicide. Despite these distractions, Wittgenstein was an utterly fearless soldier, and his exemplary bravery won him a couple of medals. (Amongst the soldiering philosophers, his only rival was Socrates.)

Wittgenstein was a parody of the driven personality. Characteristically, he saw no reason to try and alleviate this condition by searching for its cause in his own psychological make-up. On the contrary: if only everyone was true to his nature, everyone could be like this. Wittgenstein rationalized his condition to himself by claiming that life was 'an intellectual problem and a moral duty'. The intellectual and moral aspects of Wittgenstein's personality had so far remained two distinct entities, each spurring the other on. It was only during the war that they fused.

Under constant intellectual pressure (from himself), and the constant threat of death (from both the enemy and himself), Wittgenstein once again found himself in familiar territory on the brink of insanity. One day, during a lull in the fighting in Galicia, he came across a bookshop. Here he found Tolstoy's *The Gospels in Brief*, which he bought for the simple reason that there was no other book in the shop. Previously Wittgenstein had been against Christianity – this being associated with Vienna, his family, lack of a logical foundation, meek and mild behaviour, and other anathemas. But reading through Tolstoy's book was to bring the light of religion into Wittgenstein's life. Within days he had become a convinced Christian. But this conversion had a distinctly Wittgensteinian tenor. With typical rigour, he set about integrating his beliefs into his intellectual life.

Religious remarks now began appearing in the pages of his notebooks, alongside those on logic. And it soon becomes clear that these two topics have more than intellectual rigour in common. The spirit of one informs the other in compelling fashion. Even his religion had to assume a logical force and clarity: 'I know that this world exists. That I am placed in it like an eye in its visual field.' There was something problematic about the world, and this we called its meaning. But this meaning did not lie within the world, it lay outside it. 'The meaning of life, i.e. the meaning of the world, we can call God.' According to Wittgenstein, to pray was to think about the meaning of life. (Which meant that he had been praying all his life, even when he didn't believe there was a God or a meaning to life. Wittgenstein couldn't bear to be wrong – ever.)

Wittgenstein then passes on to the question of the will: an overriding element in his life, if not in his philosophy. He opens with the uncontroversial assertion that he knows his will penetrates the world. He then passes on to claim that he knows: 'That my will is good or evil. Therefore good and evil are somehow connected with the meaning of the world.' But how does Wittgenstein 'know' that his will is good or evil – and what precisely does he mean by these two terms? Also, if his will is within the world, and the meaning of the world lies outside it, it is difficult to see how they can be 'somehow connected'.

Once again, Wittgenstein seemed to consider that argument only spoilt the beauty of his striking assertions. Russell had tried to correct this bad philosophic habit, but by now he was locked away in a British prison for demonstrating against the war. Wittgenstein was to persist in this infuriating habit, which flawed his early philosophical work. But was it a drawback? Wittgenstein appeared to have an inkling of what he was up to. Making such striking assertions but leaving them devoid of blurring justification or argument gave what he said an almost oracular force. Could Wittgenstein have been more concerned with effect, rather than truth? He would have been horrified at such a suggestion. Yet there's no denying this thin but distinct thread of what looks suspiciously like showmanship, which runs through his life and work. Like it or not, his was a personality of mythical proportions (and for the most part he genuinely didn't like this). One can only assume that his propensity to back into the limelight was at least partly subconscious.

In 1918 Wittgenstein was given a commission and transferred to the Italian Front. Somehow he had managed to correspond intermittently with his beloved David Pinsent throughout the war, but he now received news that David had been killed. 'I want to tell you how much he loved you up to the last,' wrote Pinsent's mother, oblivious of the irony of her remark. (All the evidence indicates that David

Pinsent remained unaware of the true nature of his feelings for Wittgenstein, or the true nature of Wittgenstein's feelings for him.) Wittgenstein wrote back to her that David was 'my first and my only friend'. He was to dedicate his first published work to David Pinsent's memory.

In 1918 the Austro-Hungarian war effort came to an end in ignoble surrender. In Italy many of the Austrian officers simply boarded a train back to Austria, abandoning their men to their fate. But not Leutnant Wittgenstein, who would have been incapable of such an act. (It is almost impossible to exaggerate how much Wittgenstein's life was driven by principle. His moments of greatest despair always came when he temporarily ceased to drive himself to the limit, and was able to become aware of how far below his impossibly high principles his life was falling.)

When Wittgenstein was taken prisoner by the Italians, he had in his rucksack the only manuscript of the philosophical work he had been writing throughout the war. This was eventually to be called *Tractatus Logico-Philosophicus*, and is the first great philosophical work of the modern era. It is written in a series of numbered remarks. Right from its opening sentences it becomes clear that philosophy has entered a new stage. '1. The world is all that is the case. 1.1 The world is the totality of facts, not of things.'

One clear, ringing assertion follows another, linked by the absolute minimum of justification or argument: '1.13 The facts in logical space are the world. 1.2 The world divides into facts.' The book's conclusion is even more memorable: '7 What we cannot speak about we must pass over in silence.'

Few others have altered the course of philosophy in quite so striking a fashion. Such succinct perspicacity is surpassed only by Socrates ('Know thyself'), Descartes ('I think, therefore I am') and Nietzsche ('God is dead'). In the parts where it is not too technical (in the logical sense), Wittgenstein's *Tractatus* is the most exciting work of philosophy ever written. Its clarity and daring leaps of argument make it at times almost poetic, as do many of its conclusions. And its basic idea is simple to grasp.

The *Tractatus* is an attempt to delineate what we can talk about in a meaningful manner. This leads to the question: what is language? Wittgenstein claimed that language gives us a picture of the world. This idea had been inspired by a newspaper report he had read about a court case, where model cars had been used to represent an accident. The model cars were like language describing the actual state of affairs. They pictured what had happened. But most importantly they shared the same 'logical form' – they both obeyed the rules of logic. The model cars (language) could also be used to describe all possibilities (near miss, traffic jam, absence of car which was alleged to have caused the accident, etc.). But they could not describe two cars occupying the same space at once, or one car occupying two separate spaces at once. Logical form prevented this – both in reality and in language.

Language consists of pictures of reality, when it is analysed down to its atomic propositions. In this way propositions can represent the whole of reality, all facts – because propositions and reality have the same logical form. They *cannot* be illogical.

The limits of language are the limits of thought, because this too cannot be illogical. We cannot go beyond language, as to do so would be to go beyond the limits of logical possibility. The logical propositions of language are a picture of the world, and can be nothing else. They can say nothing about anything else. This means that certain things simply cannot be said. Unfortunately the assertions in the *Tractatus* fall into this category. These assertions are not pictures of the world.

Wittgenstein realized this. In trying to over-come this difficulty, he clung to his earlier idea that although certain things cannot be *said* to be true, they can be *shown* to be true. He admitted that in the *Tractatus* he was trying to say what can in fact only be shown. Though he concludes the *Tractatus* with his celebrated magisterial pronouncement which forbids others from trying the same. ('What we cannot speak about we must pass over in silence.')

Inevitably, God falls into this category of things which cannot be spoken about. We can't say anything about God because lan-guage only pictures reality. However, Witt-genstein claims that such things as God do exist: it's just that they can't be said or thought. '6. 522 There are, indeed, things that cannot be put into words. They *make them-selves manifest*. They are what is mystical.' In common with his writings in his wartime notebooks, the end of the *Tractatus* is a compelling blend of logic and mysticism. It is very difficult to dismiss this as hocus-pocus, especially when it is expressed with such forceful clarity. Unfortunately, it has to be dismissed as philosophy – though it probably qualifies as philosophic poetry of the highest order.

Sadly, there are a number of even more crucial objections to the *Tractatus*. Admittedly, language and reality certainly have some relation to one another. But how do we know that this relation is in fact 'logical form'? Wittgenstein was forced to fudge this issue. (Though he certainly didn't believe that this was what he was doing. Perish the thought. This would have been as unthinkable as a logical impossibility.) Also, the category of things we cannot talk about includes a large number of things which we simply must talk about, if we are to continue living in a civilized fashion. For a start, we can't talk about good and evil (or even right and wrong). Likewise, the 'language' of art also falls into this category, for it is in essence illogical. In being metaphorical, a work of art is both itself and something else. To say of a work of art that what it expresses is inexpressible is a contradiction. (And even Wittgenstein would find it difficult to argue that it doesn't express anything at all.) Some have even argued that language itself falls into this category. Wittgenstein overcomes this problem by declaring that since logical propositions are tautologous they do in fact 'say nothing'. This admission would appear to put an end to philosophy as such. Wittgenstein has the good grace (or overweening pride) to point this out in his preface to the *Tractatus*.

However, despite these serious objections and the admission of philosophic bankruptcy, the *Tractatus* was to have a profound influence. In particular, it proved an inspiration to the Vienna Circle, who formulated Logical Positivism. Philosophy may have come to an end, but it didn't stop the Logical Positivists from developing this end into a further philosophy of their own. According to the Logical Positivists, the meaning of any proposition lies in its manner of verification. There are two meaningful types of proposition. In the first, which are to be found in mathematics and logic, the meaning of the subject is contained in the meaning of the predicate. They are tautologous, i.e. self-evidently true, and this can be verified by comparing the subject with the predicate. For example, 'Twelve minus ten is two'. The second type of proposition is verifiable by observation, e.g., 'The ball is rolling down the hill'. If you can't verify a statement, it is meaningless. This ruled out all metaphysics, which included theological statements such as 'God exists'. According to Wittgenstein such a question as 'Does God exist?' is not only incapable of being answered, but incapable of being asked in the first place as it goes beyond the limits of logic and is thus meaningless. We simply cannot speak in any meaningful fashion about what isn't either tautologous or else verifiable by observation.

Wittgenstein put the finishing touches to the *Tractatus Logico-Philosophicus* whilst being held under conditions of extreme privation in an Italian prisoner-of-war camp at Cassino. From here he managed to make contact with Russell, and eventually the *Tractatus* was published with a preface by Russell. This preface outraged and disillusioned Wittgenstein, because he considered that it showed Russell hadn't understood his book. Wittgenstein insisted upon including his own introduction as a corrective. In this, he modestly points out that his work contains 'the unassailable and definitive . . . *truth* . . . the final solution of the problem [of philosophy]'. However, he does at least concede: 'how little is achieved when these problems are solved'.

Having put an end to philosophy, Wittgenstein quite logically saw no point in continuing with this subject. When he returned home to

Austria after the war he began looking around for another field of endeavour. He thought of entering a monastery, but considered the monk who greeted him at the gate offensively rude, so abandoned the idea and took up working as a gardener in the monastery grounds instead. He was determined to lead the life of a saint (even if his philosophy had denied the meaningful existence of saints, rendering them unspeakable). In fact, Wittgenstein was once again a deeply troubled man. As a result of his wartime conversion, he now believed in living a simple spiritual life very similar to that preached by Tolstoy during his last years.

The Austro-Hungarian Empire was in ruins, and Austria itself was bankrupt – both spiritually and financially. However, on the instructions of Karl Wittgenstein before he died the family fortune had been re-invested in America. To his son Ludwig's extreme irritation, this meant that he was now even richer than he had been before the war, when he had tried to give away his inheritance. In between hoeing the monastery garden, Wittgenstein visited Vienna to make sure that this time the family lawyer followed his instructions *to the letter* and gave away *all* his inherited fortune. This took some time, as the family lawyer at first found his instructions impossible to believe, and then found it equally impossible to believe how much he was expected to get rid of. But eventually he managed to pass on most of it to Wittgenstein's sisters, who had no wish to see any more of the family fortune frittered away on donations to other-worldly or alcoholic poets.

Having got rid of philosophy and his inherited millions, Wittgenstein decided to become a school teacher in a remote mountain village in Lower Austria. After turning down one village because it had a pleasant little park with a fountain ('This is not for me, I want an entirely rural spot') he eventually happened upon the poor village of Trattenbach.

Wittgenstein's sojourn here was a catastrophe for all concerned. With aristocratic arrogance he began inflicting his new spiritual principles upon the peasant children, and the parents were outraged. (They needed no teaching about poverty and simplicity.) The God-fearing villagers were equally outraged when their high-minded schoolmaster refused to attend church because in his opinion the sermons were spiritually vacuous. And they were even more put out when he refused to join them for a drink in the local *bierstube*, instead choosing to remain upstairs in his bare room playing the clarinet (and contemplating suicide). After a couple of years things came to a head. There was an incident at the school, in which Wittgenstein struck a child. This was blown up out of all proportion, and the villagers managed to get rid of their impossible self-appointed saint.

Wittgenstein returned to Vienna, where his family became seriously worried about his mental condition. In the end one of his sisters commissioned him to build a new house for her. Wittgenstein took on the task with characteristic earnestness, designing a modern block-like building utterly devoid of all ornamentation. But this was to be no simple construction; each element of the design had to be fulfilled with fanatical exactitude. An entire wall was knocked down when a window was found to be a few centimetres out of place, each individual doorhandle had to be purpose-built, the window latches were discovered to be aesthetically unacceptable, and so forth. The builders were driven to distraction by their perfectionist taskmaster. But they couldn't afford to leave the employ of this lunatic who was building his millionairess sister a three-storey modern residential prison, because out on the streets of Vienna people were starving.

This house still stands on Kundmangasse, a street close to the Danube canal in an eastern district of Vienna. In appearance the building is a rather unexceptional early twentieth-century modernist block, three storeys high, with rows of large plain windows. When I first located the *Wittgensteinhaus* several years ago, I was informed that it was not open to the public. Disappointedly I stood in the street, trying to peer up through the windows in an attempt to see what it looked like inside. Through one of the windows I noticed a staircase, which crossed it diagonally. After a few moments I quickly turned away. A woman had begun ascending the staircase and I had inadvertently found myself gazing up her skirt. This architectural howler had evidently been overlooked by the architect, amidst his obsession with precisely positioned and impeccably designed light switches and the like. (In a striking parallel Wittgenstein's second philosophy – which must have been forming in his mind at the time – shows remarkably similar characteristics in its obsession with detail and complete disregard for the requirements of the people who are expected to live with it.) When I last saw the *Wittgensteinhaus* some years back, it ostensibly housed the Bulgarian Cultural Institute – a concept which might not have withstood the rigorous logical analysis practised by the building's creator. In those days before the fall of the Iron Curtain the place was a nest of spies.

At the same time as Wittgenstein was building this house for his sister, he also began meeting regularly with members of the Vienna Circle. This discussion group contained some of the finest minds in central Europe, including the philosopher Schlick (who was later to be shot by a student disappointed with his exam results) and the logician Carnap (who came to believe that all philosophical problems would be solved if only we all started speaking Esperanto). The members of the Vienna Circle were in the process of developing the ideas in Wittgenstein's *Tractatus* into the virulent anti-metaphysics of Logical Positivism. They were astounded when they found that Wittgenstein himself was a deeply spiritual man. Though they should have been warned: the *Tractatus* has a prevalent strain of cryptic mysticism. ('It is not *how* things are in the world that is mystical, but *that* it exists.') By way of an explanation, Wittgenstein claimed that what he had *not* said in the *Tractatus* was much more important than what he *had* said. The best minds in central Europe listened in baffled silence as their hero attempted to explain what he hadn't said, which couldn't be said. This philosophical Indian rope trick made Wittgenstein realize that perhaps he hadn't quite succeeded in killing off philosophy after all.

This was a unique event. Never before had a major philosopher admitted, even to himself, that his philosophy was wrong. But Wittgenstein characteristically went one step further. Since his philosophy was wrong, then all

philosophy was obviously wrong. Wittgenstein now embarked on his second attempt to
destroy philosophy – once and for all.

In 1929 Wittgenstein returned to Cambridge. The only philosopher in the world who
could possibly have understood what Wittgenstein was talking about was Russell, and
it quickly became clear to Russell that he had
no idea what Wittgenstein was talking about.
But it was decided to admit Wittgenstein as a
Fellow of Trinity College all the same (despite
the fact that he hadn't even taken a degree).

Wittgenstein was to continue lecturing at
Cambridge for the next eighteen years – all the
while typically belabouring himself for doing
something so 'dishonest', and describing philosophy as 'a kind of living death'. In his lectures he began elaborating his new
philosophy: anti-philosophy. These are the
legendary lectures that were held in Wittgenstein's ascetically bare rooms, which can still
be seen in Whewell's Court at Trinity College,

overlooking a quiet little courtyard with a lawn and a bronze statue of a naked youth. The only ornament in Wittgenstein's rooms was a safe, where he kept the papers containing the philosophy that no one else could understand, in case someone stole it. The chosen few who were permitted to attend Wittgenstein's lectures were required to bring their own deck-chairs. They would sit in silence while Wittgenstein held his head 'thinking'. Occasionally, with every appearance of extreme effort, the philosopher would deliver himself of a 'thought'. With anyone else but Wittgenstein this would have been a farcically pretentious demonstration of 'original thinking'. But all present agree that the atmosphere was electric. Occasionally Wittgenstein would grill one of his 'students'. These included some of the finest minds in Cambridge, the usual lonely intellectual young men, and in later years a black US Airforceman who wandered in uninvited one day and was asked to stay because of his 'cheery face'. (Meanwhile professors from Cornell and the like who'd crossed the Atlantic to hear Wittgenstein were liable to be refused admittance.)

All are agreed that when Wittgenstein interrogated one of his students on a philosophical point, the nearest equivalent was the Spanish Inquisition. Wittgenstein had a personality of such domineering power that he reduced his audience to a state of terror. The only man who was known to have stood up to him was Alan Turing, the inventor of the computer and one of the finest mathematicians of the age (who was later forced to abandon his mathematical career to win the Second World War by cracking the Germans' Enigma code). During one of his lectures Wittgenstein suggested that a system – such as logic or mathematics – could remain valid even if it contained a contradiction. Turing disagreed: there was no point in building a bridge with mathematics that contained a hidden contradiction, or the bridge was liable to fall down. Wittgenstein wouldn't accept this: empirical considerations played no part in logic. But Turing refused to be brow-beaten, and went on insisting that the bridge would fall down. (The parallel with the application of Wittgenstein's philosophy to other fields in real life provides interesting food for thought.)

During his time at Cambridge Wittgenstein became something of a *monstre sacré* for the university. He would turn up at the weekly meetings of the Philosophical Club and monopolize the discussions, aggressively destroying the arguments of professors and undergraduates alike. He remained intensely lonely, but managed to form a few relationships with his lonely intellectual young men, one of whom he ended up living with. Wittgenstein invariably dominated these relationships, which were for the most part Platonic, but he often caused great harm to his companions. He would insist that they give up their academic pursuits and live a life of Tolstoyan simplicity – working in a local factory or becoming a hospital porter.

At the outbreak of the Second World War he too became a hospital porter. Fortunately his highly placed friends at the university had managed to secure British nationality for him, but he suffered deeply over the fact that he was safe while his sisters remained in Nazi-occupied Vienna. The Wittgensteins were Jewish, and despite being the Austrian equivalent of the Rothschilds their safety was far from assured. (Ludwig was not the only one to inherit the Wittgenstein trait of principled arrogance. When a Nazi official informed his sister that the Wittgensteins need have no fear that they would be classified as Jews, she was highly indignant. No mere upstart was ever going to tell the Wittgensteins what they were, or what they were not – and she insisted upon being issued at once with papers certifying that she was of Jewish blood.)

In 1944 Wittgenstein returned to Cambridge and began preparing for publication a manuscript containing his new philosophy. This was to be called *Philosophical Investigations*, and was finally published in 1953. This and the *Tractatus*, which he now disowned, were to be the only two books which Wittgenstein prepared for publication during his lifetime. Over half a dozen works appeared posthumously: these were made up of lecture notes taken by his 'students', and several notebooks from the famous safe.

Some have found it particularly symbolic that this safe was the only luxury which Wittgenstein permitted himself during his long ascetic period. The man who craved for clarity in both his life and work kept many dark secrets locked within him. Similarly, others have commented on the resemblance between his pronouncement 'What we cannot speak about we must pass over in silence' and his attitude towards his homosexuality. A life so intense as Wittgenstein's is bound to be rich in such parallels. But here we are perhaps better off following another of his famous remarks: 'Little that is meaningful can be said about such matters, they can only be shown.'

In comparison to the *Tractatus*, Wittgenstein's *Philosophical Investigations* is a bitter disappointment. The lucidity and daring of the *Tractatus* is replaced by nitpicking logical analysis of particular sensations and the meaning of words. There is no such thing as philosophy any more, just philosophizing – which consists of unravelling mistakes in our thinking. These arise through linguistic errors. Language is not a picture of the world, it is like a net, which consists of many pieces of interconnected string. Our understanding becomes knotted when we misuse a word in a situation to which it does not apply. The duty of philosophy is painstakingly to unravel these knots. This is why philosophy is now so complex (and so boring). The long and glorious tradition of philosophy and its profound questions which formed an integral part of our culture are now reduced to linguistic fossicking. Wittgenstein's later philosophy has recently been compared to the Superstring Theory in science, which states that the fundamental sub-atomic particles that make up the universe are like pieces of interlocking string. This comparison is false – only one of these cat's cradle theories could possibly prove interesting.

Having delineated his second philosophy, Wittgenstein set off once again for a life of solitude and asceticism. He lived for a while in a remote cottage in the West of Ireland, where he did his thinking and fed the seagulls. But he soon became too ill to live such an austere life, and began staying with various friends in England and America. Eventually cancer was diagnosed, and he died in Cambridge on 29 April 1951. His grave, with its suitably plain tombstone giving simply his name and dates, can be seen in the grassy, pleasantly unkempt graveyard of St Giles's Catholic Church (which is a mile up the Huntingdon Road from the church itself). When I visited this spot, on a cold misty February afternoon, the borders of Wittgenstein's grave had been planted by an admirer with little winter-flowering pansies (which almost certainly would not have met with the aesthetic approval of its occupant). The gravestone itself was slightly scuffed – suggesting the rather more clumsy (or possibly disrespectful) attentions of undergraduates. To this day the notorious philosophicide continues to attract his uncalled-for devotees.

Afterword

As a consequence of Wittgenstein's second philosophy, the questions once asked by philosophy have now passed into the realms of poetry. The way poetry is going, it looks as if they won't be asked much longer here either. We have learned to do without God, and it looks as if we will learn to do without philosophy. This will now, alas, join the ranks of subjects which are completed (and have become completely spurious), such as alchemy, astrology, Platonic love and stylitism.

Some key arguments

Wittgenstein opens his *Tractatus-Logico-Philosophicus* with two striking remarks:

1   The world is all that is the
           case.

1.1   The world is the totality of
           facts, not of things.

Having made these unsupported
assertions, he goes on to argue:

1.12   For the totality of facts
           determines what is the case,
           and also whatever is not the
           case.
1.13   The facts in logical space are
           the world.

This leads on to:

2   What is the case – a fact – is
            the existence of states of
            affairs.

2.01   A state of affairs (a state of
            things) is a combination of
            objects (things).

He then claims:

2.012   In logic nothing is accidental:
            if a thing *can* occur in a state
            of affairs, the possibility of the
            state of affairs must be written
            into the thing itself.

Later, he states his ethical position:

6.421   It is clear that ethics cannot be
            put into words. Ethics is
            transcendental.

(Ethics and aesthetics are one and the same.)

6.43   If the good or bad exercise of the will does alter the world, it can alter only the limits of the world, not the facts – not what can be expressed by means of language.

He reveals that his attitude is essentially mystical:

6.432   *How* things are in the world is a matter of complete indifference to what is higher. God does not reveal himself *in* the facts.

This leads him to denigrate philosophy:

6.53   The correct method in philosophy would really be the following: to say nothing except what can be said, i.e. propositions of natural science – i.e. something that has nothing to do with philosophy – and then, whenever someone else wanted to say something metaphysical to demonstrate to him that he had failed to give a meaning to certain signs in his propositions.

He then modestly denigrates his own philosophy:

6.54   My propositions serve as elucidations in the following way: anyone who understands me eventually recognizes them as nonsensical, when he has used them – as steps – to climb up beyond them. (He must, so to speak, throw

> away the ladder after he has
> climbed up it.)

This leads to his final, controversial conclusion:

> 7   What we cannot speak about
>   we must pass over in silence.
>   (from *Tractatus-Logico-Philosophicus*
>   translated by D. F. Pears
>   and B. F. McGuinness)

In his later *Philosophical Investigations*, Wittgenstein reduces philosophy to linguistic analysis:

> 30   So one might say: the ostensive
>   definition explains the use – the
>   meaning – of the word when
>   the overall role of the word in
>   language is clear. He gives an
>   example: Thus if I know that
>   someone means to explain a
>   colour-word to me the osten-

sive definition 'That is called "sepia"' will help me to understand the word. – And you can say this, so long as you do not forget that all sorts of problems attach to the words 'to know' or 'to be clear' . . .

He elaborates with a further example:

31   When one shews someone the king in chess and says: 'This is the king', this does not tell him the use of the piece – unless he already knows the rules of the game up to this last point: the shape of the king. You could imagine him having learnt the rules of the game without ever having been shewn an actual piece. The shape of the chessman corresponds here to the sound or shape of the word.

This eventually leads him to the conclusion:

123   A philosophical problem has the form: 'I don't know my way about.'

But he warns:

124   Philosophy may in no way interfere with the actual use of language; it can in the end only describe it.
    For it cannot give it any foundation either.
    It leaves everything as it is . . .

As a result, the scope of philosophy is drastically reduced:

125   It is the business of philosophy not to resolve a contradiction by means of a mathematical or logic-mathematical discovery,

but to make it possible for us to get a clear view of the state of . . . affairs *before* the contradiction is resolved. (And this does not mean that one is sidestepping a difficulty.)

This leads to a tangled situation from which it appears almost impossible to escape:

The fundamental fact here is that we lay down rules, a technique, for a game, and that then when we follow the rules, things do not turn out as we had assumed. That we are therefore as it were entangled in our own rules.

The entanglement in our rules is what we want to understand (i.e. get a clear view of).
Philosophical Investigations
(Translated by G. E. M. Anscombe)

Chronology of significant philosophical dates

6th century BC	The start of western philosophy with Thales of Miletus.
end of 6th century BC	Death of Pythagoras.
399 BC	Socrates sentenced to death in Athens.
c387 BC	Plato founds the Academy in Athens, the first university.
335 BC	Aristotle founds the Lyceum in Athens, rival school to the Academy.
324 AD	Emperor Constantine moves capital of Roman Empire to Byzantium.

400 AD	St Augustine writes his *Confessions*. Philosophy absorbed into Christian theology.
410 AD	Sack of Rome by Visigoths.
529 AD	Closure of Academy in Athens by Emperor Justinian marks end of Greco-Roman era and start of Dark Ages.
mid 13th Century	Thomas Aquinas writes his commentaries on Aristotle. Era of Scholasticism.
1453	Fall of Byzantium to Turks, end of Byzantine Empire.
1492	Columbus reaches America. Renaissance in Florence and revival of interest in Greek learning.
1543	Copernicus publishes *De revolutionibus orbium caelestium* (*On the Revolution*

of the Celestial Orbs) proving mathematically that the earth revolves around the sun.

1633   Galileo forced by Church to recant heliocentric theory of the universe.

1641   Descartes publishes his *Meditations*, the start of modern philosophy.

1677   Death of Spinoza allows publication of his *Ethics*.

1687   Newton publishes *Principia*, introducing concept of gravity.

1689   Locke publishes *Essay Concerning Human Understanding*. Start of Empiricism.

1710   Berkeley publishes *Principles of Human Knowledge*, advancing Empiricism to new extremes.

1716	Death of Leibnitz.
1739–40	Hume publishes *Treatise of Human Nature*, taking Empiricism to its logical limits.
1781	Kant, woken from his 'dogmatic slumbers' by Hume, publishes *Critique of Pure Reason*. Great era of German metaphysics begins.
1807	Hegel publishes *The Phenomenology of Mind*: high point of German metaphysics.
1818	Schopenhauer publishes *The World as Will and Representation*, introducing Indian philosophy into German metaphysics.
1889	Nietzsche, having declared 'God is dead', succumbs to madness in Turin.
1921	Wittgenstein publishes

Tractatus-Logico-Philosophicus, claiming the 'final solution' to the problems of philosophy.

1920s   Vienna Circle propound Logical Positivism.

1927   Heidegger publishes *Sein und Zeit* (*Being and Time*), heralding split between analytical and continental philosophy.

1943   Sartre publishes *L'être et le néant* (*Being and Nothingness*), advancing Heidegger's thought and instigating Existentialism.

1953   Posthumous publication of Wittgenstein's *Philosophical Investigations*. High era of Linguistic Analysis.